WHAT IS
MONEY?

First published in 2010 by Wayland

Text copyright © Claire Llewellyn 2010
Illustrations copyright © Mike Gordon 2010

Wayland
338 Euston Road
London NW1 3BH

Wayland Australia
Level 17/207 Kent Street
Sydney, NSW 2000

Senior editor: Camilla Lloyd
Designer: Paul Cherrill
Digital Colour: Carl Gordon

British Library Cataloguing in Publication Data:
Llewellyn, Claire.
What is money?. -- (Your money!)
1. Money--Juvenile literature. 2. Finance, Personal--
Juvenile literature.
I. Title II. Series III. Gordon, Mike, 1948 Mar. 16-
332'.024-dc22

ISBN: 978 0 7502 6095 4

Printed in China

Wayland is a division of Hachette Children's Books,
an Hachette UK company.

www.hachette.co.uk

WHAT IS MONEY?

Written by
Claire Llewellyn

Illustrated by
Mike Gordon

WAYLAND

We all use money from time to time to buy things like food...

...or to pay for a ride.

Money is made up of coins and notes. They come in different colours, shapes and sizes. And there are numbers on them, too.

This makes it easy to
count your money.

How much money do you have?

I get pocket money every week.

I get money on my birthday.

Sometimes money comes when you expect it. Sometimes it's a surprise.

It may be a special treat...

...or a way of saying "Well done!"...

...or maybe just a lucky find.

You always need to take
care with money because it
is very easy to lose...

...and when it's gone, you can't get it back.

So always keep your
money in a safe place.

If you have to carry it
around, make sure you
put it in a purse and ask
a grown-up to look after
it for you.

You can use your money to buy things. Before you do, think carefully about what you really want.

Sometimes you don't have enough money to buy the thing you want.

If you wait and save your money, little by little, your money will grow.

Maybe, one day, you can buy what you wanted after all.

But, remember, it's not THINGS that make us happy.

It's playing with Dad,

listening to a story,

And, luckily, times like these
are fabulous, fun and FREE!

 # Notes For Parents and Teachers

We all need to be able to manage our money and make financial decisions. The four books in the 'Your Money' series are intended as a first step along this path. Based on children's everyday lives, the series is a light-hearted introduction to money, everyday financial transactions, planning and saving and financial choices.

'What is Money?' introduces the concept of money, and familiarises readers with notes and coins. It looks at the different ways we can get money and how we use it to spend or save. It explains why we should look after our money and what happens when we lose it.

Suggested follow-up activities

• Do a survey to assess where most children get their money from. How many get pocket money? How many get presents from other family members? How many do chores for cash? Present the results as a pictogram.

• Cut out pictures of people (e.g. children, teenagers, retired people, tradespeople, professionals) from catalogues or magazines. Prepare some possible captions, explaining where each person gets his or her money from – e.g. 'I go to work every day'; 'I work on Saturdays'; 'I get money on my birthday'; 'I have a pension.' Ask children to choose the best caption for each person.

- Give children lots of different notes and coins. Allow them to familiarise themselves with them. Which is the biggest coin or note? Which is the smallest? What colour are the notes and coins? What pictures are on them? What is written on them? Can they say how much each one is worth?

- Make a collection of different currencies from around the world. What are they called? Can the children find out where they are used and mark this on a map? Do they know what they are worth?

- Make some playing cards using pictures of notes and coins. Use them to play a game of Money Snap.

- Set up a shop and ask children to stick prices on items for sale. Give them money to handle. Get them to role-play buying and selling, and to calculate change.

- Make a collection of items for your children to 'buy'. Ask them to price them at under 50p. Say that each child has £1 to spend and must choose two items. How much change will they get from their one-pound coin?

- Look for different poems and stories about money. Why not try to write one of your own?

- Money is always on the move. Can you and your child devise a story about the day in the life of a one-pound coin?

BOOKS TO READ

'Learning About Money: Saving Money' by Mary Firestone
(First Fact Books, 2004)
'Using Money' by Rebecca Rissman
(Heinemann Library, 2010)

USEFUL WEBSITES

www.pfeg.org
www.mymoneyonline.org

INDEX